Psychology and Health Series:

Volume 3

DRUGS
&
ADDICTIONS

SOME THINGS YOU MIGHT KNOW,
A LOT OF THINGS YOU MIGHT NOT.

Marios Savva

I dedicate all my books in my Psychology and Health series, to my loving family.

TABLE OF CONTENTS

THE AUTHOR

As an experienced psychologist currently living in Birmingham, England, and a member of the British Psychological Society, I now have the fervent desire to start writing books on psychology for people to read. I have endeavoured to make my books interesting to read and, with a little humour, as some psychology material can get 'heavy' and slightly complicated. DRUGS AND ADDICTIONS: *SOME THINGS YOU MIGHT KNOW, A LOT OF THINGS YOU MIGHT NOT* is the third book in the Psychology and Health series. Readers can contact me on: marios.spurs@hotmail.co.uk.

Other books by the author

Stress

Depression

Body Image

Know Thyself

I Want To Sleep

Introduction: Drugs and Addiction

Drugs are any legal or illegal substances that biochemically (biologically and chemically) affect the brain and the human central nervous system, altering perception and mood. Harmful drugs are those that are destructive to human health and are addictive. Drugs that alter perceptions and mood are called *psychoactive drugs*. There three types of psychoactive drugs:

Depressants- These calm neural activity and slow down bodily functions (alcohol, tranquillizers *or barbiturates*, and opiates such as heroin).

Stimulants- These temporarily excite neural activity, induce pleasurable feelings and arouse body functions (caffeine, nicotine, the powerful *amphetamines* or methamphetamines such as "speed", and the even more powerful *cocaine*).

Hallucinogens- These distort perceptions and evoke vivid images in the absence of input via our senses, which is why these drugs are also called *psychedelics*, meaning mind-manifesting, i.e. the mind creates it by itself (ecstasy, LSD).

Marijuana- A mild hallucinogen but which can also act as a stimulant or a depressant.

Addiction- Is the intense craving/need for a drug that develops after a period of physical or psychological (or both) dependence. Addiction has both psychological and biological aspects. Psychologically, addiction is often characterized by loss of control over the use of the substance. People who are addicted may organize their lives around getting and using drugs.

Characteristics of Addiction:

• A compulsion (something that someone believes/feels they have to do) to continue taking the drug and obtain it by any means.

• A tendency to increase the dose (due to **tolerance**). Tolerance is when the body is habituated (used to) a drug, that is, one becomes immunised to the effects, so that with regular use, increasingly higher doses of the drug are needed to achieve similar effects.

• A psychological and /or physical dependence on the effects of the drug.

• Withdrawal effect: The sickness (discomfort and distress) that users suffer when stopping the use of an addictive drug.

Some drugs are more addictive than others: The most addictive are, nicotine, heroin (and all opiates), cocaine and alcohol. The least addictive are marijuana and caffeine. But although marijuana is considered among the less addictive, if you have deep psychological needs it can become strongly addictive and continual use creates problems.

There are several theories in psychology as to why people use drugs to the point of addiction. Indeed the essential question that many experts ask is not so much as "why do you try drugs?" its "why do you continue using them?" The most common theories are as follows:

The *Biological Theory* explains that some people may be genetically pre-disposed (biologically vulnerable) to use drugs and get addicted, that is, it may be hereditary (genes passed down from parents, grandparents).

The *Behavioural Theory* explains that we as humans get conditioned to seek the pleasurable experience of using a drug, that is, we get used to that pleasure and learn to continually want to seek it. Or, on the other hand, we get conditioned to avoid the negative effects of withdrawal which often leads to severe anxiety, depression and panic.

The *Personality Theories* explain that weak personalities (impulsive, passive, defensive, low self-esteem) try to escape their problems in drugs. Such persons can become conditioned to avoid the negative effects of problems in real life.

The *Interactionist Theory* states that using illegal drugs is culturally learned: we imitate the behaviour of parents and peers. Or, that using illegal drugs requires prior contact with a drug subculture. Once someone is part of this, by sharing these outsider norms (norms are an understood rule for accepted behaviour. Norms prescribe "proper" behaviour.) it can create a strong sense of companionship, and even belonging. Generally, according to this theory, attitudes towards drugs are learnt from people around us.

These are the four main theories as to why people use drugs and indeed perhaps more importantly why they continue using them. All these theories are valid but it is more likely that there are combinations of the above theories rather than just the one being the sole cause of drug use.

This has been an introductory chapter in to the definition of drugs and addictions. In the following chapters you can find in depth information on specific drugs and drug use as well as the different aspects of addictions.

Why people use Drugs

Some People use drugs or alcohol for recreation, seeking pleasure, because their friends do, or because their parents tell them not to. Others get started with doctor's prescriptions, coffee, or their first aspirin tablet. There is another category of drug users; those who want relief from pain or suffering. Or, because they have abysses in their personality or are emotionally empty or void of feelings. Others even are seeking inner truth.

For adolescents, research points to 4 motives for drug use:

> • To expand their awareness and as a way of coping with their problems.

> • Out of curiosity, that is, to gain an understanding of what it is like to use drugs.

> • For thrill seeking and as a way to become part of the "in-group."

> • To get high and to reach a higher state of consciousness or spirituality.

Adolescents whose friends are heavy users are more likely to use drugs/alcohol. For many adolescents and teenagers, smoking and drinking stands for culturally acceptable ways for rebelliousness and maturity.

Here, I'd like to point out something important concerning the fourth motive as mentioned above concerning the heightened state of consciousness or spirituality. Drugs increase sensitivity, **not** consciousness or spirituality. Drugs cause a change in perception, in the subjective state (self-perceived happiness or satisfaction with life)- not a change in *being*, which is, incidentally, what religion wishes.

4

As I mentioned in the beginning some people smoke for recreational purposes (to have fun, to have a good time, pleasure-seeking), but by using drugs in this way they can cover their psychological needs in the mean time (deep psychological needs that most times people are not self-aware of). Consequently, the inhibitions go and addiction sets in. Thus doing drugs for recreational use to begin with, more often than not, leads to addiction, and thus the drugs become, instead of something fun to begin with, eventually necessary to survive, to endure, to cope with life- even one's self.

Once someone has started using drugs, their *tolerance* of the drug increases and this leads to more use. Tolerance is when the body is used to a drug, that is, one becomes immunised to the effects, so that with regular use, increasingly higher doses of the drug are needed to achieve similar effects. This explains why withdrawal leads to profound distress and craving, a disease that is out of control. Although the consequences of withdrawal can be severe, the wanting and craving will decline after the drug use has stopped.

The expectation of rewards from drug taking is powerful. Indeed, the learnt expectations may be more powerful than the biological properties of the substance. Drug taking is seen as adaptive since it is the individual's way of coping with stresses. It is important to note here that once drug use has ceased, the notion of craving, with the right psychological support, becomes replaced by the idea that withdrawal effects must be replaced by the idea that withdrawal effects must be understood in terms of the user's <u>expectations</u> of the *consequences* of withdrawal.

This is based on Thorndike's Law of Effect: Which, in a nutshell, states that behaviours followed by favourable consequences become more likely and behaviours followed by unfavourable consequences become less likely. Based on the Thorndike's above famous theory we can see why the "reward" from taking drugs leads to a behaviour which is typified by dependency; drugs have a relaxing and calming effect which can be very easily sought after continuously. This again reiterates Thorndike's premise: if drug use did not have this pleasurable feeling, including temporary nullifying of stress and anxiety, then there is no favourable result of taking drugs, hence no need or desperation to use them.

We shall see other common (and not) reasons for why people take to drugs in the ensuing chapters.

Marijuana: The Myth and the Reality

Marijuana (cannabis) also known as hashish, is the most widely used illegal drug. It is a naturally occurring drug made from parts of the cannabis plant. The upper leaves, tops and stems of the plant are cut, dried and rolled in to cigarettes. Specifically *hashish* ('hash') is the dried resin that seeps from the cannabis leaves and is more potent than marijuana.

It is classed as a mild hallucinogen with complex effects and contrary to popular belief, it has diverse effects on the brain and central nervous system. It can induce feelings of relaxation, elevate mood, and produce mild hallucinations.

It has been used since ancient times for its psychoactive effects and as a remedy for a wide range of medical conditions. In the 19th century, marijuana was used as much as aspirin is used today for headaches and minor aches and pains. It could be bought without a prescription in any drug store. Although marijuana may have some legitimate medical uses, such as in reducing pressure within the eyes in patients with glaucoma or treating the nausea and vomiting that often follows chemotherapy in cancer patients, research shows there are very serious consequences with long term use including becoming psychotic and schizophrenic. From the results of one psychological study, it was found that marijuana can cause impaired memory functioning as well as other cognitive impairments to the brain. Moreover, men who began using it in their teenage years were found to have smaller brains and less grey matter than other males.

Although many users report positive mood changes (even this though is not long-lasting) others experience disturbing feelings of anxiety and confusion and, occasionally, even psychotic reactions such as extreme paranoia. Some marijuana users become disorientated which can make them feel frightened or threatened. Smoking marijuana also introduces cancer-causing substances in to the body, which raises the risks of developing cancer. It can also raise blood pressure which can be serious to someone with a heart condition. Frequent use of cannabis can have an adverse effect on a man's sperm count and suppress ovulation in women, indeed; if a woman is pregnant, smoking marijuana may harm the baby.

Cannabis (marijuana) is often used with other substances, especially nicotine, alcohol, and cocaine. Marijuana may be mixed and smoked with opioids (you may read about the opioids in the next chapter), phencyclidine (PCP), or hallucinogenic drugs (you may also read about hallucinogens in chapter 6). Individuals who regularly use cannabis often suffer from physical and mental lethargy and anhedonia (feeling no pleasure at all). A large percentage of users suffer from mild forms of depression, anxiety, or irritability. When taken in high doses users can experience adverse mental effects resembling those of hallucinogens. Severe anxiety reactions can occur that resemble Panic Attacks.

Marijuana intoxication usually begins with a "high" feeling, normally followed by euphoria with inappropriate laughter and grandiosity, sedation, lethargy, impairment in short-term memory, difficulty carrying out complex mental processes, impaired judgement, distorted sensory perceptions, impaired movement, and the sensation that time is passing slowly. Sometimes, anxiety (which can be severe), dysphoria, or social withdrawal occurs. Also, increased appetite, dry mouth, and tachycardia occur as well.

It has been well documented that marijuana users can also suffer from distorted realities and de-realisation including hallucinations; seeing, feeling or hearing things that are not there i.e. have no sensory basis.

Irrelevant of the reason why someone may start smoking marijuana - for fun, a dare, to find relief from stress or psychological pain – if a user has deep psychological needs then they will continue to smoke it, they will become accustomed to using it to be psychologically at ease. As is mentioned above, long term use can have serious consequences depending on the amount used and the individual's organism. It is often the case that the "high" and the pleasant relaxation that using marijuana can give can lead, and often does, to users seeking an even more intense high or a deeper feeling of relaxation. This in turn, can lead to individuals trying harder drugs like cocaine or heroin, which, can lead to even greater consequences including the ultimate one – death. There are other healthier and more effective ways and strategies for an individual to find a sense of calm and to become more capable of coping with stress and other issues.

Opiates (Heroin)

Opiates are a class of narcotic drugs that include natural opiates derived from the opium poppy, such as morphine and heroin, and chemically similar drugs that are synthesized to produce opiate-like effects, such as methadone. Like other depressants, opioids slow down the activity of the central nervous system. Opioids have legitimate medical uses, especially relief from pain. But they are also widely abused as street drugs.

Morphine was introduced in the late 19th century in the US during the Civil War and in Europe during the Franco-Prussian War. It was freely used to deaden pain from war wounds. Physical dependence on the morphine became known as the 'soldier's disease.' *Heroin* was so named because it made people feel 'heroic'. It was also hailed as the 'hero' that would cure the physical dependence on morphine we just mentioned. Yet heroin proved to be just as addictive as morphine. Heroin can provide a strong euphoric 'rush'. Users claim that it is so pleasurable it can eradicate any thought of food or sex. Regular users develop tolerance for heroine, leading them to take yet higher doses, which can cause potentially life threatening overdoses. Heroin is usually taken by injection.

Heroin is illegal. Because the penalties for possession or sale are high, it is also expensive. For this reason, many physiologically dependent people support their habit through dealing (selling heroin), prostitution, theft, or selling stolen goods.

Opiate addicts such as heroin users face extremely unpleasant withdrawal syndromes, which may begin with flu-like symptoms and progress through tremors, cramps, chills alternating with sweating, rapid pulse, high blood pressure, insomnia, vomiting, and diarrhoea. However these syndromes are variable from one person to another and can be managed medically.

For many individuals, the effect of taking an opioid such as heroin for the first time is actually dysphoric rather than euphoric, and nausea and vomiting may result. Individuals with an opioid dependence are at risk for the development of mild to severe depression. Periods of depression are especially common during chronic intoxication or in association with other physical, psychological or social stresses. Insomnia is common, especially during withdrawal. Antisocial Personality Disorder is much more common in individuals with opioid dependence than in the general population- as is Post-Traumatic Stress Disorder.

A history of conduct disorder in childhood or adolescence has been identified as a significant risk factor for substance-related disorders, especially opioid dependence.

Heroin is also sold as 'brown'. Brown is still heroin, although some people mistakenly think it is not as addictive.

As mentioned above heroin is usually taken by injection. The risks of sharing needles and other contraptions to inject heroin are well-known, veins are often severely damaged and this has been known to lead to gangrene. There is also the very possible danger of infections like hepatitis B or C, tuberculosis and of course HIV/AIDS. Females commonly have disturbances of reproduction and irregular periods.

The risk of death from overdose increases after a period when not taking the drug because the body's tolerance for the drug decreases. Excessive doses can lead to a coma and respiratory failure as well as inhaling vomit (heroin stops the body's cough reflex working properly) can lead to death.

Accidents and injuries due to violence that is associated with buying or selling drugs is common. In some countries, violence accounts for more opioid-related deaths than overdose or HIV infection.

Opioid dependence can begin at any age, but problems associated with opioid use are most commonly observed in the late teenage years or early 20s. Once dependence develops, it usually continues over a period of many years, even though brief periods of abstinence are frequent. Relapse following abstinence is common.

Unfortunately it is not just opioid users themselves that suffer- it is also their families that suffer with them. Studies show that family members of individuals with an opioid dependence such as heroin are likely to have higher levels of psychopathology.

In closing this chapter we shall state something that is not known to many: The brain has its own natural opioids. For example, the brain secrets endorphins to blunt the feeling of pain (like the brain's own morphine). Another effect can be hyperactivity and a temporary feeling of well being. The brain's opioids are powerful numbing agents that can enable people to have a heightened tolerance for pain- an effect that has been noted by battlefield surgeons who found severely wounded soldiers needed lower doses of narcotics to handle their pain than did civilians with far less serious injuries (we mentioned the origin of heroin used in wars in the beginning of this chapter).

Amphetamines/ Methamphetamines (Speed)

Amphetamines are a group of stimulants, including methamphetamines ('speed') that were first used by soldiers during World War II to help them remain alert through the night. Truck drivers in the US and Europe have used them to stay awake all night. Students have used them to stay up for all night studies for exams the next day and people dieting have used them to quell feelings of hunger (appetite suppressants-'diet pills'). These drugs can be taken orally, smoked, snorted, or injected.

Called speed, uppers, bennies (for Benzedrine), and dexies for (Dexedrine), or ice, these drugs are often used for the euphoric 'rush' they can produce, especially in high doses. Thus, it is this twofold effect they have: they increase states of alertness and induce pleasurable feelings. Regular users may stay awake and 'high' for days on end. Such highs though inevitably come to an end. People who have been on prolonged highs sometimes 'crash,' or fall into a deep sleep or depression.

A very pure form of Methamphetamine is called 'ice' because of the appearance of its crystals when observed under magnification. Because of its high purity and relatively low vaporization point, as is true for 'crack' (a common form of cocaine), ice can be smoked to produce an immediate and powerful stimulant effect. In the US, amphetamines and other stimulants may be obtained by prescription for the treatment of obesity, Attention Deficit/Hyperactivity Disorder, and Narcolepsy. Most of the effects of amphetamines are similar to those of cocaine.

People can become psychologically dependent on amphetamines (such as speed), especially when they are routinely used to cope with stress or depression. Amphetamines are longer acting than cocaine and amphetamine use may be chronic or episodic. Aggressive or violent behaviour is associated with amphetamine dependence, especially when high doses are smoked, ingested, or administered intravenously. As with cocaine, intense but temporary anxiety resembling panic, or generalized anxiety as well as paranoia are often seen, especially with high-dosage use, as well as psychotic episodes that resembles schizophrenia. Withdrawal is often associated with temporary, but potentially intense depressive symptoms that mirror severe depression.

Tolerance to this drug, as well as to most drugs, develops rapidly and leads to substantial escalation of the dose. Recent evidence suggests that regular use of methamphetamine, a particularly powerful amphetamine, can also lead to physical dependence.

High doses of amphetamines may cause restlessness, insomnia, loss of appetite, and irritability. Amphetamine use can also induce a form of psychosis (a break with reality) which is characterized by hallucinations and delusions that mimic the symptoms of paranoid schizophrenia. Heavy use of methamphetamine - also known as meth, chalk, ice, crystal, and glass - is also linked with mental and emotional problems and with possible neurological damage. For example, research has shown that heavy use is linked to the reduction of the neurotransmitter dopamine in the brain (dopamine is involved in the experience of pleasure and reward). Persistent dopamine reduction can lead users to rely increasingly on methamphetamine to experience pleasure.

Amphetamine intoxication generally begins with a 'high' feeling, followed by the development of symptoms such as euphoria, hyperactivity, anxiety, tension, grandiosity, and anger, to name a few. With chronic use there can be sadness and social withdrawal. Physical symptoms can be tachycardia (or the opposite), elevation of blood pressure, nausea or vomiting, weight loss, respiratory problems, chest pain, and even coma.

Withdrawal symptoms ('crashing') often follow an episode of intense high-dose use (a 'speed run') and are usually characterized by fatigue, vivid and unpleasant dreams, insomnia or hypersomnia (a sleep disorder in which someone sleeps for long periods and is always very tired during the day), increased appetite, difficulties in body movement and depression. A 'crash' generally requires several days rest and recuperation and the depressive symptoms may last up to several weeks and is sometimes accompanied by suicide ideation.

Ecstasy (technically MDMA) is an amphetamine-like drug that has mild euphoric and hallucinogenic effects. Ecstasy is a synthetic drug manufactured in the laboratory. Although used by many teenagers who believe it to be a harmless way to party it poses serious physical and psychological risks. It raises blood pressure and heart rate- something which is potentially dangerous for people with cardiovascular conditions (some people are not aware they have a heart condition). Psychologically, it can cause depression, anxiety, insomnia and even psychotic features such as extreme paranoia. Studies show that the drug ecstasy damages brain cells. If you think this drug will leave you ecstatic, think again.

Some individuals, who develop a dependence on amphetamines such as speed or amphetamine-like substances such as ecstasy or abuse them, begin using them in an attempt to control their weight. Others become introduced to them through the illegal market.

Dependence can occur rapidly when the substance is used intravenously or smoked. Oral administration usually results in a slower progression from use to dependence. Amphetamine dependence is associated with two patterns of use: episodic or daily (or almost daily). In the episodic pattern, use is alternated with days of non-use (e.g. intense use over the weekend and on one or more weekdays). These periods of intense high-dose use are often associated with intravenous use and tend to end when supplies are depleted. In chronic daily use, there is usually an increase in the dose over time. Chronic use of high doses often becomes unpleasant because of the emergence of dysphoric and other negative drug effects.

Some data points to a tendency for persons who have been dependent on amphetamines to decrease or stop use after 8-10 years. This appears to result from the development of adverse mental and physical effects that come with long term dependence.

Cocaine

Cocaine is derived from coca leaves (from the coca plant). Indeed up to 1906 the stimulant cocaine was used in the production of the soft drink Coca-Cola, and was originally named after the plant. Chewing coca leaves is a practice generally limited to native populations in Central and South America where cocaine is grown.

Cocaine is a powerful stimulant. It can produce feelings of euphoria, curb hunger, deaden pain, and bolster self-confidence.

Cocaine may be brewed from coca leaves as a 'tea', 'snorted' in powder form, or injected in liquid form. It is sometimes mixed with heroin, yielding a drug combination known as a 'speedball'. Repeated snorting constricts blood vessels in the nose, drying the skin, and sometimes damaging the cartilage and nasal septum. These problems require surgery.

The potent cocaine derivatives known as 'crack' and 'bazooka' are inexpensive because they are unrefined. Crack differs from other forms of cocaine because it is dried in to small 'rocks' and is easily vaporized and inhaled and thus its effects have an extremely rapid onset.

Cocaine is a highly addictive drug that has extremely potent euphoric effects, and individuals exposed to it can develop dependence after using the drug for very short periods of time. An early sign of cocaine dependence is when the individual finds it increasingly difficult to resist using it whenever it is available. Because of its short effective duration of about 30-50 minutes, there is a need for frequent dosing to maintain a 'high'.

Individuals with cocaine dependence can spend extremely large amounts of money on the drug within a short period of time. As a result, the person using this drug may become involved in theft, prostitution, or drug dealing or may request salary advances to obtain money to purchase the drug and often finds it necessary to discontinue use for several days to rest or to obtain additional money.

Important responsibilities such as work or child care may be grossly neglected to obtain or use cocaine. As mentioned earlier, cocaine is a highly addictive drug that causes aggressive behaviour, paranoia, anxiety, depression (that can be accompanied by suicidal thoughts), panic attacks, weight loss and failure to experience pleasure from the ordinary pleasant experiences of daily life. Users mostly become psychologically dependent on the drug, using it compulsively to deal with the stresses of life.

As with almost all drugs, tolerance occurs with repeated use. Withdrawal symptoms, particularly hypersomnia, increased appetite, and depressed mood are likely to enhance craving and the likelihood of relapse.

Cocaine is a highly dangerous drug. It provokes sudden rises in blood pressure, constricts the coronary arteries and thickens the blood (both of which decrease the oxygen supply to the heart), and quickens the heart rate (tachycardia). Overdoses can result in respiratory and cardiovascular collapse, leading in some cases to sudden deaths.

Cocaine is a short acting drug, as mentioned earlier, that produces rapid and powerful effects on the central nervous system, especially when injected or smoked. When injected or smoked, cocaine typically produces an instant feeling of well-being, confidence, and euphoria. Dramatic behavioural changes can rapidly develop, especially with dependence.

Individuals with this dependence have been known to spend very large sums of money on the drug within very short periods of time, resulting in financial catastrophes in which savings or homes have been lost. Mental disturbances that occur in association with cocaine use usually resolve within hours to days after cessation of use, although they can persist for as long as a month. Erratic behaviour, social isolation, and sexual dysfunction are often seen in long-term cocaine dependence. Cocaine use can also result in HIV.

Individuals who are addicted to cocaine often develop a conditioned response to things related to cocaine, for example, developing a craving upon seeing any white powder. Indeed, this is a phenomenon that occurs with most drugs that cause intense psychological changes. This craving often leads to relapse, is hard to eradicate and can persist long after detoxification is completed.

Cocaine use is often associated with other addictions or abuse, especially involving alcohol, marijuana, heroin (a 'speedball'), benzodiazepines (pills for reducing anxiety and to aid sleep), which are often taken to reduce the unpleasant side effects of cocaine.

The age group with the highest rate for cocaine and crack use is the 18-25 year-olds.

Hallucinogens (Ecstasy, LSD)

Hallucinogens (also called *hallucinogenic drugs* or *psychedelics*) are drugs that cause sensory distortions (mainly seeing and hearing things that do not exist in reality) and hallucinations. Hallucinations are perceptions a person may have in the absence of sensation that are confused with reality. The most widely used hallucinogen is LSD ('acid').

Hallucinogens are a diverse group of substances including lysergic acid diethylamide (LSD), phenylalkylamines (mescaline, 'STP'), MDMA, also called 'Ecstasy', and DMT. Hallucinogens are usually taken orally, although DMT is smoked, and use by injection does occur.

LSD ('acid') is a synthetic hallucinogenic drug. Some users of 'acid' claim that it expands consciousness and opens up new worlds to them. Sometimes people believe they have achieved great insights while using LSD, but when it wears off they don't seem able to apply or recall these discoveries. As a powerful hallucinogenic, LSD produces vivid and colourful hallucinations. Some LSD users experience *flashbacks*- distorted perceptions or hallucinations that mimic the LSD 'trip' but occur days, weeks, or longer after usage. High doses may induce frightening hallucinations, impaired coordination, poor judgement, mood changes, and paranoid delusions.

As in all drugs **tolerance** (when the body is used to a drug, that is, one becomes immuned to the effects, so that with regular use, increasingly higher doses of the drug are needed to achieve similar effects) occurs with the use of psychedelics. And with hallucinogens, tolerance occurs rapidly due to its euphoric and hallucinogenic effects. Hallucinogen use is often limited to only a few times a week. Again, as with all drugs, 'craving' after stopping hallucinogens is well documented.

Hallucinogens may continue to be used despite the knowledge of adverse effects (e.g. 'bad trips', which are usually panic reactions or flashbacks). Some individuals who use MDMA ('Ecstasy') experience a 'hangover' the day after use that is characterized by insomnia, fatigue, drowsiness, sore jaw muscles from teeth clenching, loss of balance and headaches. Because substitutes are often sold as 'acid' or other hallucinogens, some of these effects may be due to other substances mixed in such as PCP or amphetamine. Some individuals can manifest dangerous behavioural reactions such as jumping out of a window under the belief that they can 'fly' due to lack of insight and judgement while intoxicated. These kinds of effects appear to be more common among those who have pre-existing mental disorders.

Individuals who misuse hallucinogens may or may not become dependent on them. However whatever the level of dependence, hallucinogenic intoxication has negative consequences on the user's social life, causing interpersonal problems due to the user's behaviour while intoxicated, isolated lifestyle, or arguments with friends/relatives. Also, they may repeatedly fail to fulfil major obligations at school, work or at home.

The essential feature of hallucinogenic intoxication is the presence of maladaptive behavioural or psychological changes (e.g. anxiety or depression, fear of losing one's mind, paranoia) that develop during or shortly after (within minutes or a few hours) hallucinogen use. Perceptual changes are a central part of intoxication, occurring while awake and alert. These include depersonalization, losing sense of what is real, illusions and hallucinations. Physical symptoms also develop such as tachycardia, sweating, palpitations, blurred vision and tremors.

Hallucinogen intoxication usually begins with some stimulant effects such as restlessness and nausea. A sequence of experiences then follows, with higher doses producing more intense symptoms. Feelings of euphoria may alternate rapidly with depression, fearfulness or anxiety so intense that there is a dread of insanity or death. Initial visual illusions or enhanced sensory experience may give way to hallucinations. At low doses, the perceptual changes frequently do not include hallucinations. *Synsesthesias* (a blending of senses) may result in sounds being 'seen'. The hallucinations are usually visual e.g. figures, persons and objects. In most cases, the individual knows that the effects are substance induced.

As we mentioned earlier *flashbacks* occur in long term use of hallucinogens. These may include images, flashes of colour, intensified colours, trailing images (images left suspended in the path of a moving object), after-images (a 'shadow' of an object remaining after removal of the object), and halos around objects. These usually subside after several months but can last longer. It is often the case that the person realizes that these are due to the drug and does not represent external reality, if this is not the case, the individual will likely be suffering from a psychotic disorder.

The drug group hallucinogens may be used as part of established religious practices. It appears that it is three times more common among males than among females with use starting in adolescence, with younger users tending to experience more disruptive emotions. The two most commonly used hallucinogens are LSD and MDMA ('Ecstasy'). Ecstasy pills can lead to death from dehydration because the user is continuously on edge through buckets of energy (usually dancing for hours on end).

An In-Depth Analysis of Addiction

In the second chapter we saw several main reasons in general as to why people may develop addictions. Here we shall examine this extremely important subject in greater depth. If you have not already read the second chapter, it would be good at this point to read through it before continuing to read this chapter.

People who do not have good and adaptive systems of combating pain and stress (here we mean more the emotional or psychological and not so much the physical) adopt addictions whether it is drugs or alcohol, gambling and so on. Very often, behind addictions there are hidden (or not) problems of depression and anxiety.

People can become addicted to many various substances. These include; alcohol (actually said to be the most powerful addiction), amphetamine, caffeine, cannabis (marijuana), hallucinogens, inhalants, nicotine, opioids, Phenyclidine (PCP), sedatives, hypnotics (e.g. sleeping pills), or anxiolytics (which reduce stress and anxiety). Some of these have similar features: alcohol shares features with sedatives, hypnotics, and anxiolytics. Cocaine shares features with amphetamines and amphetamine-like drugs. In many cases there can be an addiction of more than one substance together in combination which is known in psychology as *Poly-substance Dependence.*

Many prescribed medications as well as medications given without prescription can cause addictions. Symptoms generally occur at high doses of the medication and usually disappear when the dosage is lowered or the medication is stopped.

Impairments in cognition or mood are the most common symptoms associated with the intoxication of drugs, although anxiety, hallucinations, delusions, or seizures can also result. Symptoms usually disappear when the individual is no longer taking the substance, but resolution of the symptoms can take weeks or months and may require treatment. Drug addictions can also lead to *Psychotic disorder, Mood disorder, Anxiety disorder*, sexual dysfunction, and insomnia.

The essential feature of drug addiction is a group of cognitive (mental), behavioural, and physiological symptoms indicating that the user continues the use of the drug despite significant drug-related problems. A pattern of repeated use can result in tolerance (needing more and higher doses of a drug because the body has become used to the doses), withdrawal, and compulsive drug-taking behaviour. The symptoms of addiction are similar across various categories of drugs. 'Craving' (a strong drive/urge to use the drug) is experienced by most (if not all) drug users.

Tolerance, is the need for greatly increased amounts of the drug to achieve intoxication (or the desired effect) or a diminished effect with continued use of the same amount of the drug.

The degree to which tolerance develops varies greatly with the type of drug. Furthermore, for a specific drug, varied degrees of tolerance may develop due to its different central nervous system effects. Individuals with heavy use of opioids and stimulants can develop substantial (e.g. 10-fold) levels of tolerance, often to a dosage that would be lethal to a non-user. To put this in to a simpler perspective, many individuals who smoke cigarettes consume more than 20 cigarettes a day, an amount that would have produced symptoms of toxicity when they first started smoking. Individuals with heavy use of cannabis or PCP are generally not aware of having developed tolerance. Tolerance levels are also dependent on each individual's body organism.

Withdrawal is a maladaptive behavioural change, with simultaneous physiological and cognitive effects, that occurs when blood or tissue concentrations of a substance decline in an individual who had been using the substance heavily for a prolonged period of time. After developing unpleasant withdrawal symptoms, the person is likely to take the substance to relieve or avoid those symptoms, usually taking the substance throughout the

24

day beginning soon after they wake up. Withdrawal symptoms (which are generally the opposite of the acute effects of the substance) vary according to what drug is used.

There is a pattern of compulsive drug use that is characteristic of addiction. The individual may take the drug in larger amounts or over a longer period than was originally intended (e.g. continuing to use marijuana until dependent on it despite setting a limit of just one 'smoke').

The individual may express a persistent desire to cut down or regulate the use of the drug. Often an addict has made many unsuccessful efforts to decrease or discontinue use.

In many instances of drug addictions, virtually all of the person's daily activities revolve around the drug: obtaining it, using it and recovering from its effects. Important family, social, occupational or recreational activities may be given up or reduced because of drug use. The individual may withdraw from family activities and hobbies in order to use the substance in private or to spend more time with friends that also use the substances. Despite recognizing that the drug is contributing to a psychological or physical problem (e.g. severe depressive symptoms or damage to organs), the person continues to use the drug.

The key issue when dealing with drug users is not the existence of the problem per say, but rather the individual's failure to abstain from using the substance despite having evidence of the difficulty and the problems it is causing. Thus the key question when dealing with drug users when they enquire about or seek therapy is not why do you try drugs? It's why do you continue using them?

Drugs and Personality Disorders I

We all think we know what a "personality" is. It's all the characteristic ways a person behaves and thinks. Someone may be shy, very dramatic, or may be very sensitive. We tend to categorize people as behaving in one way in many different situations. For example, many of us are shy with people we don't know, but we won't be shy around our friends. A truly shy person is shy even among people he or she has known for some time; the shyness is part of the way the person behaves in most situations i.e. it is an enduring and consistent way of behaving.

We usually consider a way of behaving part of a person's personality only if it occurs in many times and places. What if a person's way of thinking and behaving causes significant distress to the self or others? What if the person can't change this way of relating to the world and is unhappy? We might consider this person to have a "personality disorder". A person with a personality disorder has personality characteristics that are inflexible and maladaptive and cause significant distress and impairment.

Personality disorders are also chronic; they do not come and go but originate in childhood and continue throughout adulthood. Because they affect personality, these chronic problems spread throughout every aspect of a person's life. If a man is overly suspicious, for example (a sign of a possible paranoid personality disorder), this trait will affect almost everything he does, including his employment (he may have to change jobs frequently if he believes his co-workers conspire against him), his relationships (he may not be able to sustain a lasting relationship if he can't trust anyone), and even where he lives (he may have to move if he thinks his neighbours are out to get him).

Although having this disorder may distress the affected person, individuals with personality disorders may not feel any distress; indeed it may be accurately felt by others because of the actions of the person with the disorder. This is particularly common with antisocial personality disorder, because the individual may show a blatant disregard for the rights of others yet exhibit no remorse. In certain cases, someone other than the person with the personality disorder must decide whether the disorder is causing significant functional impairment, because the affected person cannot make such a judgement.

We should note here that, unfortunately, people who have personality disorders in addition to other psychological problems tend to do poorly in treatment. Data from several studies shows that people who are depressed have a worse outcome in treatment if they also have a personality disorder.

The causes of personality disorders vary from genetics to childhood trauma but there is often a correlation between drug abuse and personality disorders. However, it is also important to examine what came before the other, since in some cases it is the personality disorder that leads to an increase in the abuse of alcohol and other substances. In most scenarios, conditions like borderline and antisocial personality disorders actually increase the risk of alcoholism especially during teen age and early adulthood. Before making a conclusion on how, if at all, drugs cause personality disorders, it is important to interrogate how these substances affect the brain and how these effects correlate to characteristics associated with various disorders. We now examine the relationship between drugs and Personality Disorders in more detail in the next chapter.

Drugs and Personality Disorders II

Alcohol and most drugs work by altering the rate at which impulses are transmitted from one nerve cell to another. Specialised chemical carriers called neurotransmitters are used to relay the impulses and each neurotransmitter has a specific purpose and effect. Dopamine, one of these chemicals, imparts a sensation of joy or happiness every time we do something that is helpful to the body; for example, a slight increase in dopamine levels is experienced after enjoying a good meal. However most commonly abused drugs trigger an excessive release of this neurotransmitter, flooding the brain with the feel good sensation. This results in addiction since, the individual will want to experience the sensation over and over again.

Continuous use of drugs results in tolerance for the neurotransmitter, meaning that more of the substance is required to achieve the same result. In most cases of drug addiction, the user finds it hard to get into a good mood without the use of a certain substance and at times the result is a sense of withdrawal from social situations. In severe cases, Schizoid or Paranoid tendencies may become noticeable leading to an alteration in personality. It is also not uncommon for individual in such a state to show signs of aggression, disobedience or indifference.

Addiction and mental illness are however, not synonymous. People with drug addiction often recover after undergoing various rehabilitation processes and at times the effects of drug use are reversed, leading to a complete recovery. In cases of personality disorder, more deep rooted factors are the cause and at times, most afflicted persons have to live their whole lives with the disorder. The characteristics of drug addiction quite often resemble those of persons with mental illness and it is at times becomes difficult to distinguish between the two. However, it is important to note that the extended abuse of certain substances can lead to personality disorders, especially when no active steps are taken to resolve the addiction. This is commonly caused by an addiction-induced, irreversible imbalance in brain functionality.

In order to establish a definitive confirmation of an existing personality disorder, a series of diagnostic parameters have to be identified and this often happens after the successful treatment for drug addiction.

There are several identifiable causes of personality disorders, and these include chemical imbalances in the brain or other neurological factors, genetic inheritance and even dysfunctional early childhood development. It is however, difficult to decisively conclude that drug abuse directly causes personality disorders. However it is also not prudent to completely rule this out as a cause. Nevertheless there is solid evidence that indicates an increased risk of drug and substance abuse among individuals with personality disorders. In the case of borderline personality disorder, which is characterised by mood swings, depression and a general sense of introversion, alcoholism and drug addiction is common.

Some studies have shown that about 12% of cocaine and alcohol users display borderline tendencies. Other conditions like antisocial, avoidant and schizoid Personality Disorders have also been associated with increased use of drugs and subsequent addiction. In some situations, the knowledge that one has a personality disorder drives the individual to use drugs in order to try and raise their spirits.

Mostly, it is an intense feeling of loneliness and depression associated with a specific condition, which leads to substance abuse. A major problem arises due to this, since substance abuse, agitates and increases symptoms associated with personality disorder. Feelings of self-loathe increase due to excessive drug use and this may lead to higher chances of the individual inflicting self-harm or even committing suicide. When it comes to treating personality disorders, various therapeutic methods have been used and it is often quite important to also treat the co-existing addiction to alcohol and other substances.

The relationship between addiction and personality disorders is incontestable, but the question as to whether or not addiction is a direct cause of personality disorders, is one that requires a more thorough and systematic interrogation by psychologists and other researchers in similar fields of science.

Withdrawal- An Addict's Worst Nightmare

When discussing the matter of withdrawal we need to reiterate what we have said about drugs and addictions to provide the context for the discussion on withdrawal.

Drug addiction is perhaps one of the most disturbing challenges of modern times. This is an issue that has struck at the very core of society destroying families and bringing with it war, crime and destitution. In The U.S. it is currently estimated that over 23 million people use drugs on a regular basis, with a significant portion of this group being strongly addicted to alcohol and other controlled substances. This large number of users contributes generously to a global drug industry that generates over 400 billion dollars every year, a figure that roughly translates to about 1% of global trade. For those running these illicit empires, unimaginable fortunes stand to be made, but for those on the receiving end, a grim future soon follows.

When discussing drugs and substance abuse, it not only includes illegal or controlled drugs, but also encompasses prescription medication and alcohol. According to the Drug Enforcement Administration's fact sheet, controlled substances are divided into 4 major groups, depending on their chemical composition and mode of action. These groups are; a) Narcotics, which include heroine, morphine and oxycodone among others, b) Depressants including barbiturates, benzodiazepines and many others, c) Stimulants, including cocaine, amphetamines and methamphetamines and d) Hallucinogens, which include some commonly abused drugs like Ecstasy, LSD, Steroids and cannabis, which is the most extensively used illegal drug in the world. Apart from these major categories, there are other drugs of interest, most of which are prescription medicine like painkillers and sleep medication.

As we mentioned, a complete reliance on drugs and a strong compulsive desire to use them in order to perform day to day tasks is defined as addiction. However, there are numerous definitions of what addiction is, and this depends on which professional you ask. At times, addiction is even considered to be a mental disorder especially when the affected person totally loses control as a result of excessive or prolonged use. The feeling of euphoria or bliss achieved when a person uses a drug for the first time often becomes the motivator for recurrent use.

Different drugs have varying modes of action but quite often, the general mechanisms by which addiction happens is similar for most substances. A drug induced alteration of neural or brain chemistry can result not only in mental disruptions but also in dependence on the causative drug. This is often referred to as **psychological dependence**. Drugs like cocaine, heroin, and marijuana often result in this type of addiction. Some normal day to day biological processes taking place in the body are also greatly affected by drug use.

Prolonged use of various substances often results in a progressive disruption of these physiological processes and ultimately, this causes tolerance. The onset of tolerance means, as we mentioned, that the affected person will have to use more and more of the drug, in order to attain the desired high. Once this happens, it is referred to as a physical or physiological dependence and is a consequence of biological adaptation by the body as it adjusts to the constant presence of drugs. An excessive reliance on alcohol leads to this sort of addiction. Currently, drug addiction is not a preserve of adults, and sadly, it is not uncommon to find children as young as 12 years of age, who are already dependent on one substance or the other.

When an addict is denied access to drugs, or if they abruptly stop using them, an array of symptoms follow and this is referred to, as we have mentioned earlier, withdrawal. Withdrawal symptoms may be mild or hardly noticeable but in most cases they often result in violent ailment. Withdrawal only occurs in persons that have a psychological or a physiological dependence on drugs and each substance has its own unique symptoms. For example, withdrawal from alcohol can result in tremors, excessive perspiration, an irritable demeanour and even nausea.

Opium derivatives like heroine and morphine cause withdrawal symptoms that include diarrhoea, vomiting and at times, and depression. The list of signs and symptoms is rather lengthy but it appears that shaking and nausea are common in most cases. An important factor that can lead to variation in symptoms is the method of drug use. For instance, injectable drugs can cause serious venous and tissue damage resulting in feverish symptoms.

Before an addict is taken off drugs, a medical practitioner needs to be consulted and the activity has to be carried out under specialized conditions. The reason for this is that some withdrawal effect can be quite harsh and at times even fatal. Severe alcoholism is an example that stands out, and withdrawal from this has been known to be fatal. In cases where the addict is pregnant, withdrawal from drugs like opiates can actually lead to loss of the infant, a situation technically referred to as foetal withdrawal.

The different phases of drug withdrawal are often a cause for alarm, and understanding them is important, especially when dealing with addicts. Going "cold turkey" is a term that has been coined for these different phases and it refers to the roller-coaster effect of withdrawal symptoms.

During the initial stages of rehabilitation, the symptoms begin to appear and subsequently build up slowly over time, becoming progressively severe. Before the peak phase of withdrawal, some patients can become quite violent in an attempt to escape the authority or situation that is keeping them away from the drugs. Other patients can become gravely ill and at times even require emergency medical attention. After hitting the plateau stage, the symptoms start to dissipate and eventually, over a period of time, the patient gets better.

Once the worst is over, it is imperative that a former addict is kept away from substances and any triggers that may cause a relapse. A trigger can also cause the re-occurrence of some withdrawal symptoms resulting in a burning urge to use. For example, the trigger for a recovering nicotine addict can be the smell of cigarette smoke which may lead to a craving for the same. The importance of keeping away from triggers cannot be overstated and it is one of the key support pillars for a recovering addict.

Drug Abuse and Addiction in Adolescents and Teenagers

Despite the numerous and awe inspiring gains achieved by mankind over countless millennia, the world today is still a very hectic place to grow up and live in. Children born in to this so called new age are faced by challenges that were unfathomable a century ago. We are used to global problems such as child mortality, rampant cases of illiteracy among children who should be in school and many other problems that often afflict the youth as they develop. However, the world's younger population is now faced with a new and more destructive reality; wide spread drug abuse and addiction.

The period of transition from childhood to adulthood is particularly sensitive. This period is known as adolescence and it typically begins around the age of 14. Individuals at this age are also referred to as teenagers, and the rates of drug abuse in this particular phase are shockingly high. Surveys carried out by the National Institute on Drug abuse show that most teenagers usually start off by consuming alcohol because of easy availability. Although this might not seem like a great cause for alarm, it is estimated that about 50% of adolescents who consume alcohol, have a high likelihood of using stronger drugs in future, or developing alcohol dependence later on in life.

An important factor to investigate is what drives teenagers to use drugs. An obvious answer would be peer pressure, but although this is a major reason, there are other more subtle factors. Ease of access to drugs is a key enabler for teenagers and especially those living in households were alcohol and other substances can be found in accessible areas. Adolescents are also well known for their tendency to rebel for no logical reason. This often comes not only from physical and hormonal changes during this age, but also from the sources of information and entertainment that teens are exposed to. With this rebellion comes an urge to engage in risky activity like using illegal drugs or binge drinking, in an attempt to either fit into a certain social grouping or just to get attention.

In cases where an adolescent has low self-esteem, they are more likely to use drugs in order to feel a sense of acceptance from peers. The perception that some risky habits are "cool" is another reason why drug use has particular allure to persons of this age group. Adolescence comes with a lot of pressure and expectation form various social circles; this brings with it stress and is often another reason for teens to self-medicate.

Presently, it is not uncommon to find drug dealers roaming around schools or even students who actually sell drugs to their co-students within school premises. This ease of access creates a situation where teenagers can get their hands on drugs whenever they please. Marijuana is currently the most accessible illegal drug for persons of this age and although the use of illegal drugs among teenagers is on the decline, other substances like prescription medication are easily available.

The use of drugs like methamphetamines and ecstasy is also rampant especially during the so called "raves" that teenagers love to attend. Some parental habits also play a role in enabling access to drugs, for instance, parents who give their teenagers overly generous allowances or pocket money, create a situation where drugs can be purchased easily, used, and even distributed.

The ability to identify various characteristics among adolescents who may be using drugs is important, especially if an early intervention is to be made. Although short term or experimental use may be a bit difficult to identify, prolonged drug use by adolescents often leads to noticeable changes in behaviour and eventually to addiction. A sudden loss of interest in academics or a sharp drop in grades, coupled by other factors like mood swings, withdrawal from social encounters and a general sense of introversion could be indicators of drug use.

Adolescent drug addicts may also result to stealing finances from the household in order to fund their habits. In extreme cases, teenagers have been known to engage in violent crime and gang activity in order to easily access the drugs they are hooked on. Once some of these characteristics are observed, the individual's parent or guardian should approach the matter with a sense of understanding and calmness with an aim of resolving the problem and not being judgemental or aggressive.

Apart from a tendency to turn to crime and adverse effects on education, drug addiction has other dire consequences for adolescents and quite often, the person's immediate family suffers considerably. This particular age group is prone to substance addiction, at times leading to irreversible emotional and psychological damage.

The effect of drug addiction on the developing adolescent brain disrupts neural connections eventually leading to impaired reasoning capacity and perception. Some of these effects can stay with the individual for life affecting future relations and prospects. It is estimated that more than 50% of teenagers who learn about drug use and addiction from their parents, eventually stay clean and do not use. It is therefore imperative for parents and guardians to impart this important knowledge on a topic that is sometimes considered to be taboo. However, for adolescents who are already using, and those who are addicted, other urgent and effective interventions need to be taken. Family and friends need to be involved in the process, and it is important to note that patience is key. When adolescent addicts are confronted with the issue, they tend to be aggressive and defensive; therefore, it is important to come up with an intervention strategy that will be acceptable to all. Although some parents fear the eventuality of a rehab facility, this option should always be considered, especially in cases where the addiction is severe.

It is important to note that the intervention process does not stop after rehabilitation. Close relatives and friends of the affected teenager should offer support after the process to avoid the possibility of relapse. Making the affected individual feel accepted and forgiven for past wrongs is also important since it creates a sense of comfort.

 # Afterword

We have mentioned in this book that some drugs are more addictive than others. If someone has deep psychological needs, drugs, even the supposedly milder ones, like marijuanas can become strongly addictive and continual use creates problems.

We also stated that some people use drugs or alcohol for recreation, seeking pleasure, or because their friends do, others get started with doctor's prescriptions. We noted another category of drug users; those who want relief from pain or suffering, or because they have abysses in their personality or are emotionally empty or void of feelings. Others even are seeking inner truth.

Whatever the origin, once an individual becomes addicted to drugs, it is very difficult to stop, especially with the harder drugs like cocaine, and contrary to how good someone may feel while taking them, drug use causes many problems on a psychological, physical and social scale. We detailed the serious consequences of drug use and addictions.

If there is one message to be concluded from this book it is this: If your using drugs, it is imperative you try and stop- <u>Now</u>. If you're thinking or feeling tempted about trying drugs- <u>Don't</u>.

I hope you enjoyed this book.

The Psychology and Health series

Stress: We Can Master It.

Depression and Sadness: Never Lose Hope – Even If You Can't See Any.

Drugs and Addictions: Some Things You Might Know, A lot of Things You Might Not.

Body Image: How We See Ourselves and Others; How This Can Lead to Problems.

Know Thyself: The Eternal Struggle of The Heart and Mind.

I Want to Sleep: Why We Struggle to Sleep – How We Can Remedy It.

www.ingramcontent.com/pod-product-compliance
Lightning Source LLC
Chambersburg PA
CBHW070230290526
45789CB00004B/1563